Power Networking for Small Businesses

How to Navigate Networking Events Like a Pro

Ellen M. Huxtable, MBA

Power Networking for Small Businesses

Copyright © 2019, Ellen M. Huxtable

ISBN: 9781070873008

CONTENTS

1 WELCOME!

Whether you've had some experience in networking, extensive experience, or are totally new to the game, welcome!

Do you eagerly look forward to networking opportunities, or does the thought of walking into a room full of strangers send your stomach into roller coaster mode? Do you strategically plan to maximize the impact of your networking activities, or do you tolerate networking events as a necessary evil? Whatever your comfort or enthusiasm levels may be, read on and identify tactics to network more effectively and represent your business in the best possible light.

You can network in person, online, or both. This book covers face-to-face networking, and strategic uses for online resources. The two modalities are complimentary, and both are valuable in building business connections.

Developing a professional network is critical to business. Business is a team sport, and your network is your extended team. There is power in numbers, strategic partnerships, and connections. Networking can create the relationships to help your business survive and thrive.

2 THE ROADMAP

Where do we begin, what is our destination, and how are we getting there?

There is nothing mysterious about networking. It is a process built from basic components. There are many approaches; everyone has their own path to success.

This book features one system, consisting of six manageable steps.

- We start with **Mindset**. If you're on the apprehensive end of the emotional spectrum, this section is especially for you. Getting you mind wrapped around the process can go a long way toward success. And if you're a networking pro, use this section to refresh your purpose and perspectives.

- Next is **Preparation**. Being prepared radically improves the probability of successful outcomes. Pay attention to details. They can take your activity to a new level.

- Dive into **The Event.** Most networking opportunities follow a standard pattern. Know what to expect, and navigate events smoothly and effectively.

- Maximize the impact of **The Conversation.** Get the most from the time you spend with new contacts.

- **After the Event** there's followup, expanded networking, and staying connected. Networking doesn't end when you leave the room; the process is just beginning. Know how to capitalize on the time and effort you've invested in the networking process.

- Nothing will happen unless you take action, so **Step Out!** Networking is a marathon, not a sprint. Be consistent and committed to the process. The advantages are great; don't miss opportunities to create and maintain business connections.

3 MINDSET

What Kind of Networker Are You?

Are you a nervous networker?

Do you shudder at the thought of mingling in a crowd? Are networking events too chaotic, too noisy, too confusing and too intimidating?

Take heart. You don't have to be the life of the party or the star of the show. Not everyone needs to be a powerhouse. You don't have to be something or someone you are not.

But someday, you might decide to step out, and meet new people, some of whom might be really interesting, and some of whom might be the perfect match for you and your business. Be assured, you can do it, and do it well. Understanding the mechanics and the networking process can go a long way toward creating confidence. Knowing what to expect and how to react can transform a scary experience into a unique opportunity. Learn how the game is played, and when you're ready, step forward and step out.

Are you a plugger?

Do you dutifully make the never-ending rounds of almost identical events? Have you lost count of the number of boneless chicken breasts in mystery sauce with rice pilaf and sautéed vegetables you've eaten at networking luncheons? Has your networking devolved into a series of comfortable conversations with old friends rather than a strategic exercise to support and grow your business?

If you're a plugger, consider the economics. Every networking event represents a financial investment, as well as a significant time commitment. The financial investment may be nominal or great, but your time is a valuable, limited, and irreplaceable resource. What return are you getting from your investment? Effective networking can boost business. Are you wasting your networking opportunities?

<u>Are you a networking pro?</u>

Are you an experienced networker? Do you attend events, make new connections and incorporate them into an established process?

Take stock. Are your systems as effective as possible? Are you taking full advantage of new strategies and new technologies? What opportunities are you missing? How can you fine tune your activities? Small changes can make a big difference. Evaluate your processes, incorporate new concepts, and boost your networking impact.

Networking for the Greater Good

In some circles, networking is viewed as being pushy, self-serving, manipulative and sleazy. And, as practiced by some, that reputation is valid. But it doesn't have to be. indeed, for those who understand the process, networking is far removed from that stereotype.

So if networking isn't necessarily sleazy, slimy and self-serving, what is it? What is its potential? Can it be a genuine force for good? Absolutely.

At is finest, networking is a forum for giving, supporting others, and making genuine connections. Its true power, for participants and for the greater community, lies in the capacity for doing well by doing good.

So as a participant, how do you stay on the noble path, and avoid sliding into the dark side? How do you maximize your impact for good, and the impact of your networking activities?

It's a matter of focus.

Real power networking is not about you; it is about them. "Them" are the people you meet networking, the people you can help, and the greater community. Focus on helping the people you meet. What are their needs? What is their pain? Far beyond what you are selling, how can you be of genuine assistance to them? Think first about them. Act without expecting any return. Be a conduit for good.

Power networking creates genuine relationships where each can offer from their strengths and benefit from the strengths of others. The network, as a whole, is greater than the sum of its parts. Build your network and empower your business.

4 PREPARATION

Have a Marketing Strategy

Networking is marketing. Before you begin, know the answer to the two key marketing questions: Who is your target customer, and why are you the best choice for them? This is the message you need to consistently send, not only in your networking activities, but also in your overall marketing efforts.

Who is your target customer?

"I sell to everyone," is not a useful marketing statement. Marketing to everyone is marketing to no one. None of us have the time, money or other resources to engage and persuade the whole of humanity. Think it through, and define your target market as narrowly as possible. Focus you resources for maximum impact. If you are a business-to-business provider, your targeted industries, locations, and size are key factors. If you are selling to consumers, financial position, age, gender, family status, geography, ethnicity, interests and hobbies are some of the basic considerations.

If you are selling to businesses, carefully consider not only the industry and business parameters, but also who within the organization is your true target customer. In a smaller business it might be the owner; in a larger organization the decision maker might not be the president or CEO, but could be anyone from a vice president to a purchasing agent to part-time summer help. Specifically define and profile not only the target company, but also your targeted decision-maker.

Your business-to-business targeted customer profile might read, "I sell to privately owned businesses in light manufacturing, with from $20 to $50 million in sales, and a full-time sales force. The purchasing decision for my product is typically made by the CEO who is the adult son or daughter of the founder, although the founder typically approves all major purchases."

In the business-to-consumer sector, the statement, "I sell to families," is too broad to define a target market. Instead, consider, "I sell to families in affluent suburbs, who are newer homeowners, with dual incomes and children in elementary school. The parents are engaged in community programs and are supportive of their children's activities, including travel team sports. They attend galas and donate to fundraisers for arts organizations. They have dietary restrictions, including gluten-free and vegetarian. They typically are in their mid-thirties, and have elderly parents who are retired and live independently, out of state."

A targeted statement brings clarity to your marketing and your networking.

Once you identify your true target customer, analyze them. Where do they hang out? Are they at chamber of commerce events, or trade shows? Are they at business luncheons or at professional association meetings? Are they at mothers' club gatherings or garden clubs? Select the right venues to network with the people you want to meet.

Why are you the best choice for them?
Consider your target customer's pain points. What is their greatest pain, and how can you relieve it? Draw from the profile you created and align your marketing message to resonate with their most significant needs.

Know and communicate the reason you are the best choice for your targeted customer. "Customers will buy from me because I really care," is a trap to successful marketing. Every one of your competitors says exactly the same thing. That's baseline; you need more. You need to stand out from the crowd. What is your unique qualification? What is your "wow" factor? How will you capture the attention of your customer? What product and approach will position you as the unqualified best choice, the only choice, for your target customer?

Take time to think this through. Have a crystal clear picture of your targeted customer or client. Know where to find them, and know what networking venues are likely to be most productive.

Analyze their motivations and needs, develop your unique offering and knockout message, and incorporate these into your networking and elevator pitch.

Your Elevator Pitch

Once you have identified your target customer and set your marketing position, it's time to craft your elevator pitch. The elevator pitch is a brief statement of what you offer and why you are the best possible choice. It is so named because it is meant to be something you can share with a fellow occupant during an elevator ride.

In the past, the typical time allotment for an elevator pitch was approximately three minutes, or a fairly reasonable elevator ride. Times have changed, and today's expectation is that your elevator pitch is from 15 to 30 seconds. This is enough time for a trip of possibly one or two floors on a reasonably fast elevator, which equates to one or two very concise sentences. Your goal is to craft one or two short sentences which focus on your product, and include a "wow!" factor which makes you memorable.

Focus your pitch on how your product relieves your customers' pain points. Be emotional. Paint a mental picture of peace and joy. Don't start the conversation talking about what your product is; talk about what it does.

To continue with the example of the suburban family mentioned earlier, if you sell dietary restricted cooked meals delivered to homes, your elevator pitch might be, "I help busy families with dietary restrictions create dinnertime memories."

Keep your statement short and simple. The purpose of the elevator pitch is to generate questions. Leave room for your listener to want to know more. Every listener will have a different response to your pitch. Some will know a lot about your product line, others will know little. Some will be intrigued by your "wow" factor, others will launch into detailed questions about the specific features you're offering. Let them guide the conversation. Diving into details which are irrelevant to them is a waste of your time and energy.

Get Ready to Rock

You have your mindset, and your focus, and your elevator pitch is perfect.

It's time to equip. Think of what you need, before you need it. Arrive at the networking venue ready to rock. Being prepared will help you present professionally, and also go a long way toward decreasing anxiety. You might not know the people, or exactly where to find the venue, but you'll know that you have your stuff.

Take an ample supply of business cards. If you're in the market to have some printed or reprinted, get cards with a matte finish, at least on one side. Have space on the matte side(s) where you or your contact can write a brief word or two. Your networking contact might want to make a note of what you're looking for, or what you offer, or some other reminder. Make sure they have a place to do so.

Have a pen that writes. Actually, have a pen and a spare. Pens tend to run dry at the most awkward times.

Take a small notepad for miscellaneous notes. If your new acquaintance doesn't have a business card, you can ask them to write their contact information for you.

Have a professionally made name tag, with your name in large print, and wear it visibly. It does no good if it's under a jacket, lapel or scarf, or in the glove compartment of your car. Many venues have adhesive name tags; these tend to get wrinkled and fall off, and are a general nuisance. Look professional and make it easy for others to see your name.

If possible, have pockets. At least two easily accessed pockets are nice. Keep your business cards in one, and put the cards you collect in the other. Also, your pen and notepad can be pocketed for quick retrieval. A purse or professional tote can also work, however it can be a bit more difficult to get the items you need, when you need them.

Dress to fit the occasion and your industry. The owner of an auto repair shop can probably dress less formally than a high-end wealth manager. Practice your handshake. Avoid the handshake extremes of bone crushing vise and wimpy dead fish. Practice smiling. Relax. Be genuine. Fake smiles are obvious and creepy.

Be prepared, and rock.

5 THE EVENT

So Many Choices

The number and variety of networking opportunities are endless. Choose your events wisely. You don't have the time to attend every gathering, and the costs for tickets and luncheons can quickly add up.

- Explore events offered by local chambers of commerce. Often these are open to non-members for a slightly higher fee.
- Online platforms such as meetup.com can direct you to relevant meetings and groups in your area.
- At events, ask other attendees where else they network. Most people active in the business community belong to several different groups;

take advantage of their knowledge. A word of caution - unless the information is offered by them, it may be awkward asking someone in your field about other networking opportunities. Some individuals can be uncomfortable sharing their resources with those they see as competitors.

Assess each opportunity. Who are the likely attendees? How much time is there to network? Does the setup lend itself to networking? What travel time is required? What is the cost?

Every event has possibilities. You can be surprised by making a great connection in the least likely of places. Don't discount or ignore the low probability venues, but don't devote all of your time to them, either.

Network frequently. Include recurrent events. These give you an opportunity to become familiar with the attendees, and give the attendees the opportunity to learn more about you. Include new groups and gatherings. You never know what group can become a strong supporter for your business.

Some networking groups or events offer opportunities for participants to make presentations. If this is an option, consider taking advantage of it. Some groups expect presentations that are informational only and not promotional; other groups are comfortable with a presentation promoting your business. Understand the expectations of the group. Being a presenter allows you to share your areas of expertise, and introduces you to the entire group at once.

Be purposeful in your networking activity, and spend your time and resources effectively.

Know the Dance

Networking, like ballet, is a dance. In ballet, every performer knows the right moves, and when to make them. Performances are choreographed to avoid collisions. There are set expectations. Networking is the same.

There is a predictable routine to virtually all networking events. There are the right moves, and the appropriate times to make them. Avoiding collisions is important. Knowing the dance can boost your confidence and improve you effectiveness.

Typically, a networking event has a check-in table. Stop and introduce yourself. There may be instructions given, such as a table assignment, or a general timetable for the gathering.

The first part of a networking event is often set aside for open networking. This is the time in which attendees mingle, greet friends and acquaintances, and introduce themselves to people they don't yet know. This is the part that, for many, is terrifying. If you are among the terrified, don't run for the hills just yet. Specific tactics to survive and thrive during this portion of the event are covered in upcoming sections.

Drinks and food are often part of the deal. Rule number one: if alcohol is offered, avoid it, or be moderate. You want to be fully functional. Most importantly, you don't want to create an impression on others that you can't remember the next day.

If there are appetizers, keep in mind that you are there to make connections, and food is secondary. Hunkering down alone in a dark corner with a loaded plate is not what the event is about.

At a luncheon or dinner, as with many events, a tipped chair, or napkin over a chair, or drink at a place indicates that that seat is taken. Unless the event is booked solid, look for a table which is already partially occupied. You don't want to be the first person or even the second to sit at table, only to find no one else joins you. Find a seat with interesting looking people and ask if a seat is available. If so, sit, smile, and introduce yourself. Start with small talk. The venue, or the weather, are stock opening lines. Connect with table mates on both your left and right. Even if one is delightfully engaging and the other responds with singular grunts, do your best. Take full advantage of the opportunity to meet both individuals.

If there is room to cruise to the other side of your table, do so. Soon after you are seated, take your business cards, go to the people at the far side, and introduce yourself. This can be far more effective than trying to shout introductions over a floral centerpiece. Share your name and business name; this isn't the time for a long elevator pitch. Hand out your card and accept theirs, if offered. Get back to your seat before food arrives; you don't want to get in the way of the wait staff. When food arrives, eat small bites; take small sips. It's easier to keep a conversation going if you have less to swallow.

If there is a speaker, they may be open to meeting attendees after the presentation. On occasion, a speaker may be less than cordial, but most presenters are approachable. Thank them for their presentation, and mention any specific shared interests. Give them your business card and accept theirs. Be brief, and don't monopolize their time. If you do have something substantive to share, email them later with a short, friendly note.

Leave the event with a handshake and a "Nice meeting you" to those around you. If there is a host, and they are available, approach them and thank them for the event.

Know the dance, and move like a pro.

Maximize Your Impact

Focus maximizes impact. Networking events can provide a change of scenery and in some cases a nice lunch you didn't have to prepare for yourself. But keep focused on your purpose. You're there to meet new people, and refresh existing relationships. Standing in a corner gingerly holding a coffee cup, or sitting alone at a table pretending to be engrossed in an urgent text message is not going to advance your cause.

Make the most of every networking opportunity. This does not mean acting like a stereotypical desperate used car salesman on the last day of the month. It does mean purposely engaging and making genuine connections with others.

Arrive early. Use all the time available for the event. As an early arrival, you'll be one of a select few. Take advantage of the opportunity to chat with the organizers, and if needed, pitch in to help with last minute details.

Whether or not you arrive early, introduce yourself to the hosts or organizers, and thank them for coordinating the event. The hosts probably know most of the attendees, and may be of assistance in helping you connect with specific individuals. And everyone appreciates a sincere word of thanks.

Say hello to your friends, take a minute or two to catch up, but focus on meeting new people. Your friends are already allies for your business; find new allies.

Make genuine contact. Your goal is quality, not quantity. Two or three new acquaintances are more important than a whole pocket full of business cards from people you can't remember. If you can't remember them, they don't remember you, either.

Stay for a bit after the official end of the event. Arrange your schedule so you have the time to take advantage of a possible late-in-the-game conversation. Make small talk with other attendees as you leave the venue. Even a "Have a nice day!" makes a positive impact. Smile and brighten someone's day.

Take full advantage of every networking event, keep focused, and work to advance your business.

6 THE CONVERSATION

Start the Conversation

You can go to a networking event, looking your best, and primed to graciously receive all comers. You stand aside, waiting for the networking magic to happen. You envision a stream of Prince and Princess Charmings will find you, introduce themselves and sweep you into fascinating and profitable conversations.

Or not.

No matter how glowing your personality, networking is an activity. Being present is important, but maximizing your effectiveness requires action. If you are depending solely on Mr.

or Ms. Charming to make the first move, you may find yourself painfully alone at the dance.

Do not expect the Charmings to miraculously materialize. YOU are responsible for your networking success. You are the one who controls your networking destiny. It's your responsibility to take the initiative and introduce yourself to the interesting people you want to meet. You will be proactive, step forward, and make the magic happen. Right? RIGHT!

If you're a networking pro, stepping forward is as natural as breathing. But sometimes, even you aren't up to full power. Scale back. Dial down the intensity. Pause and enjoy the event. See who happens to pass your way; make small talk. Connect. You might discover that sometimes, less is more, and your less intense self remains an effective networking presence.

And if you're not a networking pro, if you'd much rather wait for the Charmings to find you, be brave. See the truth. Like a fairy godmother, you have the power. Use it. You, too, can be a Charming. Do you see that individual standing alone and looking lost? They need you. Your purpose is to reach out to them. That person WANTS to meet you. Actually, they want to meet anyone, but you will be more than acceptable. They attended this shindig to meet people, and are hoping against hope that someone steps up.

YOU are that someone. So how do you make the magic happen?

Fake it until you make it. Take a deep breath, put on your biggest smile, walk over with purpose, extend your hand and say, "Hi! I'm (your name here.)" They will shake your hand and respond "Hi, I'm (their name here.)" Ask them what they do, be ready with your elevator pitch, and you're off and running.

Congratulations, you've created a win-win. You have made the gathering worthwhile for that person, and, in turn, you're reaping the benefit of a new acquaintance.

Introducing yourself to a total stranger can seem daunting, but it doesn't have to be. Remember, your purpose is to help others. So smile, step up, be a Charming, and connect with confidence.

How to Join a Conversation

Sometimes you might spot the most fascinating person or persons at a networking event. You'd love to meet them, but they're deeply engaged in conversation in a small group. What can you do?

First, if the conversation is between two people only, feel for the vibe. If the conversation is intense and focused, the duo are probably colleagues working through details of a project or deal. If this is the case, don't interrupt.

Groups of three or four, or duos engaged in light conversation not only don't mind your interest; they often are fervently wishing that someone would join their circle. Think about it. All of you are there to meet new people. The people in the group have already spent time connecting. They would love to be introduced to someone new, like, for example, you. By joining in, you are doing them a favor.

But how do you do it? How do you get noticed by the animated and talkative people in a grouping?

You hover.

In any group of standing individuals, there is a gap between people which is larger than the others. To join a group, stand just outside the group, in the gap. Look at whoever is talking; smile and nod when appropriate. Soon someone in the group will acknowledge you. When that happens, smile, extend your hand, and introduce yourself. Each person in the group will introduce themselves; shake hands with each.

Once in, should someone else look to join the group, be courteous, acknowledge them and add them to the group. You're on your way to being a networking all-star!

Ask, Listen, Talk.

You've made your move, introduced yourself, and are face-to-face with an individual or group of fellow networkers. Now what?

There is a strategy to a networking conversation. Your goal is to learn as much as possible about the other person or people, before you say anything about yourself.

People are there to meet people. After the initial handshake and sharing names, it's perfectly acceptable to ask, "What do you do?" This is the invitation for them to share their elevator pitch.

Listen carefully and sincerely. Comment supportively. If you know nothing about their industry, this is a great time to learn more. Ask questions. Keep your comments brief. Your goal is to keep the focus on them and learn as much as possible before you talk about yourself.

People usually like talking about themselves, and relate positively to someone interested in their story. Most importantly, however, the more you know about them, the more you can tailor your comments to fit their interests.

If they mention kids, grandkids, dogs or hobbies, discuss those. Talk about things you have in common with them, like your human or furry babies, or shared hobbies. Sharing interests outside of business creates connection.

They will usually stop at some point and ask what you do. If they don't, after listening to them for awhile, it is perfectly acceptable to give your elevator pitch. Tie your comments to what you know about them. When the ask questions elaborate. Be positive, engaged and energetic.

Consider the casual networking conversation as the beginning of a professional relationship. The impression you make and the information your new acquaintance will remember is based on what they see and hear. Be real. Smile. Put your best self forward.

Give.

Networking is not about you; it's about them. Yes, you are networking for a purpose - to make connections, expand your circle of influence and eventually build your business. But counterintuitively, the most effective way to get what you want is to make every effort to help others get what they want and need.

Have a giving mentality. Listen for the interests and needs of the other person. How can you help them? What resources can you suggest? Offer what you can. Ask for their business card, and make a note of what they're looking for. If you know of a website or software package or another networking group that might be useful to them, suggest that information. Be sure to write a note to yourself to follow up.

A giving mentality establishes connection. It positions you as someone who understands community. People tend to try to help those who are trying to help them.

During your discussion, give them your business card, and share information about your target market. Encourage them to contact you if you can be of assistance to them or others in the future.

Remember, your networking contact also has their own elevator pitch, and their own reason for networking. Be gracious and respect that real networking is a dialogue. Give your elevator pitch, listen to theirs, and use this information to create a meaningful conversation and connection.

Avoid the hard sell. Networking is just the beginning of a professional relationship. People need to know you, like you, and trust you before engaging your services or purchasing your products. Sometimes the process moves quickly and smoothly; at other times it can take weeks or even years for your new acquaintance to become a customer.

A special note: Frequently, people who network are seeking introductions to potential power partners, referral sources or clients. A word of caution - exercise discretion. Offer to connect individuals only when it is a win-win for both parties. Don't make a referral unless you know that the potential client or customer is actively searching for that service or product. Yes, there are some services that technically anyone can use, but unless there is current interest, you're wasting the time of both individuals and not helping either one. Subjecting your network contacts to unwanted solicitations damages your credibility and erodes your relationships.

Look for opportunities to give. Try to help those you meet, and establish your reputation within the networking community.

Determine Next Steps

Some people you meet will be a natural fit - you can materially help them and/or they can help you, and offer to do so. Others will be people with whom you want to stay in touch. You're in related fields, but there is not a current match between your offerings and needs. Still others will be interesting, but not at all in fields, industries or markets relevant to you.

Consider and communicate the next steps in your relationship. If there is no fit between your target interests and theirs, at least you've learned something about their field, and enhanced your general knowledge. Networking time is never wasted. Thank them for their time, and let them know you appreciated the opportunity to learn more about their interests and industry. Let them know you will keep them in mind, if you hear of something that is a match for them. Occasionally you'll be surprised; that the next person you meet IS the perfect match for them. In that case, get the two together on the spot, make a quick introduction and leave them to pursue the relationship.

For those who are in related fields, with the potential for future synergies, suggest a connection on LinkedIn and other professional profiles. Get their business card and make a note of the reasons you want to stay connected.

Make definitive plans with your best fit contacts. If you can help them, offer to do so. When appropriate, suggest a follow-up meeting in the office or over coffee. Be respectful of their time; suggest a meeting only if there are specific opportunities and synergies to explore.

If you have a blog or send out an email newsletter, ask if your new acquaintance would like to be added to your email list. While some individuals add everyone they meet to their email lists, it is far more gracious and professional to ask first. Having permission to email them gives added opportunities to maintain and nurture the professional relationship.

Networking is a marathon, not a sprint. Do not be discouraged if your efforts fail to yield spectacular and instantaneous results. Build your network for the long haul. Value all the connections you make. You cannot predict who you might be able to help, or who might be able to help you in the future.

Moving On

One of the potentially awkward parts of networking is moving on. You've had a good conversation with someone or a group, and have covered all the bases. You've spent a respectable amount of time, and given them your full attention. You're looking to meet other people, and you need to break away. How do you do so, gracefully?

Thank your new acquaintance or the group for taking the time to speak with you. Re-state any promises you made to connect them with resources or send information. Tell them you're looking forward to any connections or assistance they offered. If appropriate, you can state that you're looking forward to seeing them at a future event. Shake hands and tell them you enjoyed the opportunity to meet. This provides closure, and enables you to move on without appearing abrupt. Smile and move on to make your next connection.

Breaking away is a natural part of networking. If you have given your full attention to the people you have met, they will appreciate the opportunity to pursue other contacts as well.

7 AFTER THE EVENT

Follow Up

You've successfully navigated the networking event, have made new connections and briefly touched bases with old acquaintances. And your work has just begun. The networking event is only the beginning of the process.

Networking is about creating relationships, and one chance meeting at an event does not create a relationship. Take your cards and notes, and enter them into a database. Know who you met, when and where you met them, what you discussed, and their interests, both in business and in their personal lives. Send invitations to connect on LinkedIn and Facebook, and any other professional platforms you use.

Send a brief email note to your best fit contacts. Thank them for taking time to discuss their business, and ask to stay in touch. Follow up on the promises you made. Forward information and make introductions.

One efficient format for making business introductions is the joint email. Address an email to the two people you want to connect. Offer a sentence or two about each person. For example, "Joe, I'd like to introduce Fred. I met Fred at a networking event and he has purchased property for an earthworm farm. Fred, I'd like to introduce Joe. I know Joe from church, and he is active in a natural and organic farming initiative. I think you will enjoy meeting. Please feel free to contact each other directly."

Set or confirm dates for any meetings you discussed.

Developing professional relationships is an ongoing exercise. Keep in touch. If you don't follow up, you have wasted much of the potential from networking.

Expanded Networking

Networking is not and should not be confined to business events. Network everywhere, with everyone.

Hairdressers, beauticians and barbers, for example, are superb networking contacts. Does your go-to person know about your business and the potential customers and contacts you're seeking? Share your elevator speech and a few details. You never know who might overhear your conversation, or who might be telling your barber the next day that they're desperately looking for a business like yours. Leave behind a few business cards. Expand the concept, and engage all your professional acquaintances in your network.

Do you have children or grandchildren who participate in sports or extracurricular activities? Get to know the parents of their teammates. Share parenting notes. You and they have great commonalities. Indeed, some of them might become lifelong personal friends. When you have established a comfortable relationship, ask what they do "in real life," that is, when they're not cheering on the team. Listen and connect. If appropriate, ask if they have a business card, give them your card, offer to keep them in mind, and ask them to keep you in mind.

Do the people in your life know what you do? Or do your relatives and neighbors say, "I think they work for some big company," or, worse, "Gee, I've known them for years and I'm not sure what they do." You don't have to be pushy. When you're together, mention something innocuous that happened at work, a cute story or reference. For example, "The Dells must be really popular this year. Three people from the shop floor are taking their vacations there." Beyond potentially starting a conversation about the Dells, you've planted the idea that you work somewhere with a shop. If people ask, give a brief version of your elevator pitch.

If you are just as clueless about their professional life as they are of yours, ask them to fill you in. As with business networking events, learn as much as you can about them before you offer information about your business. Enjoy the exchange of information; it's fun to learn more about those who are close to you. You may be surprised to find opportunities for mutual benefit you never realized existed.

Staying Connected

Maintain top-of-mind awareness with your key contacts. Keep them in mind, stay in touch, and make it easy for them to keep you in mind as well.

What notes did you make about their business or interests? As you find articles they might enjoy, forward these to them. Don't swamp their inbox; an occasional note every few weeks, which is on target and engaging, carries far more positive impact than three spammy emails every day.

For those you have connected with on LinkedIn and Facebook, use the birthday and business anniversary reminders to maintain contact. Rather than using the default greetings, take a few extra seconds to personalize the message before sending it.

Review your LinkedIn and Facebook profiles. Make sure they are current and present you professionally. Post a recent picture and comment on your current activities. Make it easy for someone to find you on social media, and identify you from the potentially dozens of people with your same name.

Create a professional page for your business on both LinkedIn and Facebook. Keep the pages current. Have a website and keep it current, as well. New acquaintances with whom you have commonalities will be curious about you and your company. Their first instinct will be to google your name and company, to learn more. Be easy to find.

Google your name and your company's name. Do any questionable listings come up? If so, try to neutralize them with more current information that presents you and your company in a more positive light. Be aware of reviews, especially those which are not complimentary. Respond to comments, whether they are positive or negative.

You have a responsibility to be your own best advocate. If you have won an award, or engaged in a charitable activity, mention that in social media. While social media postings only reach a fraction of your contacts, positive news is always worth sharing.

Follow local business publications and applicable trade journals and organizations. Scan them for the names of your networking contacts, and use messaging in social media to congratulate them. If they are mentioned in printed media, clip the article or picture and send it to them with a brief note.

For those with whom you've made an ongoing connection, and with whom you want to stay in touch, invite them to coffee. This is not a sales or marketing opportunity, but rather a time to catch up on both business and personal developments. How did their son's baseball tournament turn out? Did they buy the new technology they were considering? Extend the offer meet, but don't force the relationship. Sometimes the timing isn't right, but a future offer may be perfect.

The goal of networking is to create and build ongoing professional relationships. Networking events are the first step in a continual process. Your network is built by sustaining, strengthening and nurturing the contacts you made, face-to-face.

8 STEP OUT!

The Payoff

Face-to-face networking requires an investment of time and resources. Your goal is to spread awareness of your business, and maintain a top-of-mind presence among your professional associates. Ideally you will ultimately derive customers or clients from your networking efforts, but benefits can extend far beyond the obvious.

In the small business marketplace, in-person visibility is critical. The people you meet through networking learn not only about your business, but more importantly, get to know about you, as a person. As you develop professional relationships through repeated contact, people are developing comfort with and confidence in both you and your business. Networking creates an ever-expanding cohort of allies with the potential to connect you to future power partners and customers.

Regardless of your industry, your network is an invaluable resource. Business is a team sport, and your business network is your professional team. Share your expertise, and call upon your network when they have expertise you lack. No one knows everything; no one is an expert in everything. Your network expands your expertise and effectiveness, and you, in turn, can expand the expertise and effectiveness of others in your network.

A note on professionalism - utilizing your network does not mean expecting free services, products or advice. Respect the expertise and value of your networking contacts. Pay for the goods and services you request. If a discount or complimentary service is offered, accept graciously, and make every effort to reciprocate when the occasion arises.

Nothing lasts forever. Over time, there will be subtle but cumulative changes in your network. Some changes will strengthen your network; others will erode your connections. Some people will build their business or be promoted within a corporation. Others may leave the area, dissolve their business or make a major transition. You may have a great referral source, who is lured away by a competitor, or the perfect power partner may materialize from nowhere. Your business network is a dynamic system. Work continuously to build and maintain your contacts. Stay in touch with those you have met.

Face-to-face networking is an invaluable skill and resource. Practice it, hone your capabilities and be the best advocate for your business.

Just Do It!

Talk is easy and cheap. All the theory in the world is not effective unless applied in real life.

If you're already a power networker, consider incorporating a new idea or two, and boost your activity to new levels. Assess what works for you, and continuously develop your systems to meet your evolving needs.

For those more apprehensive or less experienced, proceed at your own pace. Use this information as a guide. As you become more familiar with networking activities, they will become more routine, predictable and comfortable.

Revisit the sections of this book which fit your needs. Add your own marginal notes. Take one step at a time. Move forward, and celebrate your successes.

Networking skills are a powerful tool in your marketing arsenal. Develop them and expand your professional capabilities and effectiveness.

Go ahead. Step out. Network like a pro. Build and support your business! Just do it!

ABOUT US

About Advantage Business Concepts

Advantage Business Concepts helps business leaders address critical issues and accelerate business growth. We offer presentations on a range of business topics, facilitate internal teams and peer advisory groups, and offer direct consultative services.

About the Author:

Ellen Huxtable, the owner of Advantage Business Concepts, is an instructor for the Small Business Development Center, Waubonsee Community College, and has made presentations for the Women's Business Development Center, the Medical Group Management Association, the Aurora University Sales Institute, and numerous other organizations. Ellen hosts Batavia Spotlight, a business program for BATV public television. She serves on the Board of Directors for the Cavaliers Drum and Bugle Corps, and the Community Advisory Board for the Fermilab National Accelerator Laboratory. Ellen holds a MBA from the Kellogg School of Management, Northwestern University.